THE **TESTING** SERIES

POLICE OFFICER APPLICATION FORM
QUESTIONS & ANSWERS

THE **TESTING** SERIES
expert advice on test preparation

how2become

Orders: Please contact How2become Ltd, Suite 2, 50 Churchill Square Business Centre, Kings Hill, Kent ME19 4YU. You can also order via the e-mail address info@how2become.co.uk and at Gardners.com.

ISBN: 9781907558689

First published 2012

Typeset for How2become Ltd by Molly Hill, Canada.

Printed in Great Britain for How2become Ltd by Bell & Bain Ltd, 303 Burnfield Road, Thornliebank, Glasgow G46 7UQ.

WELCOME

Welcome to *Police officer application form questions and answers*. This guide has been designed to help you prepare for the initial stage of the tough police officer selection process

The selection process to join the police is highly competitive. Approximately 65,000 people apply to join the police every year. What is even more staggering is that only approximately 7,000 of those applicants will be successful. You could view this as a worrying statistic, or alternatively you could view it that you are determined to be one of the 7,000 who are successful. Armed with this workbook you have certainly taken the first step to passing the police officer application form.

The guide itself has been split up into useful sections to make it easier for you to prepare. Read each section carefully and take notes as you progress. Don't ever give up on your dreams; if you really want to become a police officer then you *can* do it. The way to approach the police officer selection process is to embark on a programme of in-depth preparation and this guide will show you exactly how to do that.

The way to pass the police officer application form is to develop your own skills and experiences around the core competencies that are required to become a police officer. Many candidates who apply to join the police will be unaware that the core competencies even exist. As you progress through this guide you will find that these important elements of the police officer role will form the foundations of your preparation. So, the first step in your preparation and before we go any further, is to get hold of a copy of the police officer core competencies. They will usually form part of your application pack but if they don't, you can obtain a copy of them by visiting the website of the force you are applying to join.

If you need any further help with any elements of the police officer selection process including role play, written test and interview then we offer a wide range of products to assist you. These are all available through our online shop www.how2become.co.uk.

We also run a 1-day intensive Police Officer Course. Details are available at the website

WWW.POLICECOURSE.CO.UK

Once again, thank you for your custom and we wish you every success in your pursuit to becoming a police officer.

Work hard, stay focused and be what you want...

Best wishes,

The how2become team

The How2become Team

INTRODUCTION

The application form is the first stage of the selection process for becoming a police officer. During this section I will provide you with a step-by-step approach to completing a successful application. It is important to point out that I have used a number of the more common types of application form questions within this section and it is your responsibility to confirm that they relate to your particular form. I have deliberately not made reference to any sections of the form that relate to personal details, simply because what you write here is based on you and you alone.

Whenever I have completed application forms in the past I have always set aside plenty of time to give them justice. I would recommend you allow at least five evenings to complete the form, breaking it up into manageable sections. Many candidates will try and complete the form in one sitting and as a result their concentration will wane and so will the quality of their submission.

You will be asked a number of questions on the application form and on the following pages I have provided you with some tips and advice on how to approach these questions. Please remember that these are provided as a guide only and you should base your answers around your own experiences in both work life and personal life. Questions that are based around 'knowledge, skills and experience' are looking for you to demonstrate that you can meet the requirements of the 'person specification' for the job you are applying for. Therefore, your answers should match these as closely as possible.

Your first step is to find out what the 'person specification' is for the particular force you are applying to join. Essentially, the role of a police officer is made up of a number of core competencies. You may receive these in your application pack or alternatively they can usually be found on the main police recruitment website, or on the website of the force you are applying to join. Whatever you do, make sure you get a copy of them, and have them by your side when completing the application form. Basically you are looking to match your responses with the police officer core competencies.

Once you have found the 'core competencies', now is the time to structure your answer around these, ensuring that you briefly cover each area based upon your own experiences in both your work life and personal life.

The core competencies that form the basis of the police officer role are similar to the following. Please note that the core competencies do change from time to time so it is important to confirm that they are correct.

RESPECT FOR RACE AND DIVERSITY

This essentially involves considering and showing respect for the opinions, circumstances and feelings of colleagues and members of the public, no matter what their race, religion, position, background, circumstances, status or appearance. You must ensure that you are aware of how important this is to the role of a police officer.

TEAM WORKING

Police officers must be able to work in teams as well as having an ability to work on their own, unsupervised. In order to meet this core competency you will need to be able to develop strong working relationships both inside and outside the team. If there are barriers between different groups then you will need to have the skills to break them down and involve other people in discussions and decisions that you make.

COMMUNITY AND CUSTOMER FOCUS

As a police officer you must focus on the customer. The customer is essentially the members of the public whom you will be dealing with. You will need to be capable of providing a high-quality service that is tailored to meet each person's individual needs.

The only way that you can provide a high quality service to the public is by understanding the needs of your community. Once you understand the needs of your community then you will be able to provide an excellent service.

EFFECTIVE COMMUNICATION

Police officers must be able to communicate both verbally and in writing. You will also need to communicate to the people you are addressing in a style and manner that is appropriate. This can sometimes be difficult, but with practice, it can be achieved.

As a serving police officer you will be required to take accurate notes of incidents that you attend. Therefore, the Police Force that you are applying to join will want to assess your potential in this area during the written tests element of the selection process.

PROBLEM SOLVING

In order to solve problems effectively you will first need to gather sufficient information. This can usually be achieved through a number of sources. For example, if as a police officer you were investigating a burglary, you would first want to gather witness statements from the owner of the property and also the owners of surrounding properties. This information may then lead to other information sources, which will allow you to gather sufficient evidence to make decisions that will ultimately lead to the problem being solved through effective decision-making.

PERSONAL RESPONSIBILITY

Police officers have a reputation for getting things done. They are very good at taking personal responsibility for making things happen and achieving results. In order to effectively achieve this you will need to display a level of motivation, commitment, perseverance and conscientiousness. At all times you will need to act with a high degree of integrity.

RESILIENCE

As a police officer you will do doubt be faced with difficult and pressurised circumstances. It is during these tough situations that you will need to show resilience. For example, imagine turning up to a 999 call where a group of drunken lads are refusing to leave a pub after closing time. How would you deal with the situation? You must be prepared to make difficult decisions and have the confidence to see them through.

Now that we have taken a brief look at the core competencies, we can start to look at some of the application form questions. But before we do this, take a read of the following important tips, which will help you to submit a first class application.

- Make sure you read the whole of the application form at least twice before preparing your responses, including the guidance notes.

- Read and understand the person specification and the police officer core competencies.

- Try to tailor your answers around the 'core competencies' and include any keywords or phrases you think are relevant.

- Make sure you base your answers on actual events that you have experienced either in your work life or personal life.

- Fill the form out in the correct ink colour. If you fail to follow this simple instruction then your form may end up in the bin!

- Follow all instructions carefully.

- If there is a specific word count for each question, make sure you stick to it.

- Make sure you keep a photocopy of your completed application form before sending it off as you could be asked questions relating to it during the interview stage if you progress that far.

- Do not lie.

- Get someone to read your practice/completed application form to check for spelling/grammar mistakes. You lose marks for poor grammar/spelling.

- Finally, send your application form recorded delivery. This will prevent your form going missing in the post, which happens more often that you think.

SAMPLE APPLICATION FORM QUESTIONS AND ANSWERS

DISCLAIMER: the responses that are contained within this guide are not to be copied or duplicated in any manner; they are for illustration and guidance purposes only. It is vital that you complete your own form using answers to the questions that are based on your own unique and individual circumstances. All characters, incidents and situations appearing in this work are fictitious.

The following sample application form questions may not be applicable to your specific form. However, they will provide you with some excellent tips and advice on how to approach the questions.

SAMPLE QUESTION NUMBER 1

What knowledge, skills and experiences do you have that will enable you to meet the requirements of a police officer?

ANSWER (EXAMPLE ONLY)

"In my previous employment as a customer services assistant I was required to work closely with the general public on many occasions. Often I would be required to provide varied solutions to customers' problems or complaints after listening to their concerns. It was always important for me to listen carefully to what they had to say and respond in a manner that was both respectful and understanding.

On some occasions I would have to communicate with members of the public from a different race or background and I made sure I paid particular attention to making sure they understood how I was going to resolve their problems for them. I would always be sensitive to how they may have been feeling on the other end of the telephone.

Every Monday morning the team that I was a part of would hold a meeting to discuss ways in which we could improve our service to the customer. During these meetings I would always ensure that I contributed and shared any relevant experiences I had had during the previous week. Sometimes during the group discussions I would find that some members of the group were shy and not very confident at coming forward, so I always sensitively tried to involve them wherever possible.

I remember on one occasion during a meeting I provided a solution to a problem that had been on-going for some time. I had noticed that customers would often call back to see if their complaint had been resolved, which was often time-consuming for the company to deal with. So I suggested that we should have a system where customers were called back after 48 hours with an update of progress in relation to their complaint. My suggestion was taken forward and is now an integral part of the company's procedures. I found it quite hard at first to persuade managers to take on my idea but I was confident that the change would provide a better service to the public we were serving."

First of all read the example answer we have provided above. Then try to 'match' the answer to the core competencies that are relevant to the role of a police officer and you will begin to understand what is required.

For example, the first paragraph reads as follows:

"In my previous employment as a customer services assistant I was required to work closely with the general public on many occasions. Often I would be required to provide varied solutions to customers' problems or complaints after listening to their concerns. It was always important for me to listen carefully to what they had to say and respond in a manner that was both respectful and understanding."

The above paragraph matches elements of the core competency of community and customer focus.

Now take a look at the next paragraph:

"On some occasions I would have to communicate with members of the public from a different race or background and I made sure I paid particular attention to making sure they understood how I was going to resolve their problems for them. I would always be sensitive to how they may have been feeling on the other end of the telephone."

The response matches elements of the core competency of respect for race and diversity.

Hopefully you are now beginning to understand what is required and how important it is to 'match' your response with the core competencies that are being assessed. Remember to make sure you read fully the guidance notes that are contained within your application pack. You will also hopefully start to realise why I recommend you set aside five evenings to complete the form!

It is also possible to use examples from your personal life, so don't just think about work experiences but look at other aspects of your life too. Try also to think of any community work that you have been involved in. Have you been a special constable or do you work for a charity or other similar organisation? Maybe you are a member of neighbourhood watch and if so you should find it quite a simple process to match the core competencies.

Try to tailor your responses to the core competencies that are being assessed and briefly cover each assessable area if possible. You may also want to try to include keywords and phrases from the core competencies when constructing your response.

I have now provided a number of sample keywords and phrases that are relevant to each core competency. These will help you to understand exactly what I mean when I say 'match' the core competencies in each of your responses.

KEYWORDS AND PHRASES TO CONSIDER USING IN YOUR RESPONSES TO THE APPLICATION FORM QUESTIONS

Respect for race and diversity

- Show respect for others
- Take into account the feelings of colleagues

Team working

- Develop strong working relationships
- Achieve common goals
- Break down barriers
- Involve others

Community and customer focus

- Focusing on the customer
- High-quality service
- The needs of others
- Understand the community
- Commitment

Effective communication

- Communicates ideas
- Effective communication
- Understand others

Problem solving

- Gather information
- Analyse information
- Identify problems
- Make effective decisions

Personal responsibility
- Take personal responsibility
- Achieve results
- Motivation
- Commitment
- Perseverance
- Conscientiousness
- Act with a high degree of integrity

Resilience
- Make difficult decisions
- Confidence

Now let's move on to some more sample application form questions and responses.

SAMPLE QUESTION NUMBER 2

Why have you applied for this post and what do you have to offer?

Some Police Force application forms may ask you questions based around the question above. If so, then you need to answer again in conjunction with the 'person spec' relevant to that particular force.

An example answer for the above question could be based around the following:

"I believe my personal qualities and attributes would be suited to that of a police officer within this Constabulary. I enjoy working in a diverse organisation that offers many and varied challenges. I would enjoy the challenge of working in a customer-focused environment that requires a high level of personal responsibility, openness to change and teamwork. I have a high level of commitment, motivation and integrity, which I believe would help the Police Force respond to the needs of their community."

Top tips

- The length of response that you provide should be dictated by the amount of space available to you on the application form or the specified number of maximum words.

- The form itself may provide you with the facility to attach a separate sheet if necessary. If it doesn't then make sure you keep to the space provided.

- The best tip I can give you is to write down your answer first in rough before committing your answer to paper on the actual application form. This will allow you to iron out any mistakes.

SAMPLE QUESTION NUMBER 3

It is essential that police officers are capable of showing respect for other people regardless of their background. Please describe a situation when you have challenged someone's behaviour that was bullying, discriminatory or insensitive. You will be assessed on how positively you acted during the situation, and also on how well you understood what had occurred.

PART 1 - DESCRIBE THE SITUATION AND ALSO TELL US ABOUT THE OTHER PERSON OR PEOPLE WHO WERE INVOLVED.

"Whilst working as a sales person for my previous employer, I was serving a lady who was from an ethnic background. I was helping her to choose a gift for her son's 7th birthday when a group of four youths entered the shop and began looking around at the goods we had for sale.

For some strange reason they began to make racist jokes and comments to the lady. I was naturally offended by the comments and was concerned for the lady to whom these comments were directed.

Any form of bullying and harassment is not welcome in any situation and I was determined to stop it immediately and protect the lady from any more harm."

Top tips

- Try to answer this type of question focusing on the positive action that you took, identifying that you understood the situation. Don't forget to include keywords and phrases in your response that are relevant to the competencies that are being assessed.

- Make sure you are honest in your responses. The situations you provide MUST be real and ones that you took part in.

PART 2 - WHAT DID YOU SAY AND WHAT DID YOU DO?

"The lady was clearly upset by their actions and I too found them both offensive and insensitive. I decided to take immediate action and stood between the lady and the youths to try to protect her from any more verbal abuse or comments. I told them in a calm manner that their comments were

not welcome and would not be tolerated. I then called over my manager for assistance and asked him to call the police before asking the four youths to leave the shop.

I wanted to diffuse the situation as soon as possible, being constantly aware of the lady's feelings. I was confident that the shop's CCTV cameras would have picked up the four offending youths and that the police would be able to deal with the situation.

After the youths had left the shop I sat the lady down and made her a cup of tea whilst we waited for the police to arrive. I did everything that I could to support and comfort the lady and told her that I would be prepared to act as a witness to the bullying and harassment that I had just witnessed."

Top tip

- Remember to read the core competencies before constructing your response. What are the police looking for in relation to what you say to others and how you act?

PART 3 - WHY DO YOU THINK THE OTHER PEOPLE BEHAVED AS THEY DID?

"I believe it is predominantly down to a lack of understanding, education and awareness. Unless people are educated and understand why these comments are not acceptable then they are not open to change.

They behave in this manner because they are unaware of how dangerous their comments and actions are. They believe it is socially acceptable to act this way when it certainly isn't."

Top tip

- When describing your thoughts or opinions on how others acted in a given situation, keep your personal views separate. Try to provide a response that shows a mature understanding of the situation.

PART 4 - WHAT WOULD HAVE BEEN THE CONSEQUENCES IF YOU HAD NOT ACTED AS YOU DID?

"The consequences are numerous. To begin with I would have been condoning this type of behaviour and missing an opportunity to let the offenders know that their actions are wrong (educating them). I would have also been letting the lady down, which would have in turn made her feel frightened, hurt and not supported.

We all have the opportunity to help stop discriminatory behaviour and providing we ourselves are not in any physical danger then we should take positive action to stop it."

Top tip

- Try to demonstrate an understanding of what would have possibly happened if you had failed to take action.

SAMPLE QUESTION NUMBER 4

Police officers are required to work in teams and therefore they must be able to work well with others. Please describe a situation when it was necessary to work with other people in order to get something done and achieve a positive result. During this question you will be assessed on how you co-operated with the other members of the team in completing the task in hand.

PART 1 - TELL US WHAT HAD TO BE DONE.

"Whilst driving along the motorway I noticed that an accident had just occurred up in front of me. Two cars were involved in the accident and some people in the car appeared to be injured. There were a number of people stood around looking at the crash and I was concerned that help had not been called.

We needed to work as a team to call the emergency services, look after the injured people in the cars and try to stay as safe as possible."

Top tip

- Make sure you provide a response to the questions that is specific in nature. Do not fall into the trap of telling them what you 'would do' if the situation was to occur.

PART 2 - HOW WAS IT THAT YOU BECAME INVOLVED?

"I became involved through pure instinct. I'm not the type of person to sit in the background and let others resolve situations. I prefer to try to help out where I can and I believed that, in this situation, something needed to be done. It was apparent that people were hurt and the emergency services had not been called yet.

There were plenty of people around but they weren't working as a team to get the essentials done."

Top tip

- It is better to say that you volunteered to get involved rather than that you were asked.

PART 3 - WHAT DID YOU DO AND WHAT DID OTHERS DO?

"I immediately shouted out loud and asked if anybody was a trained first aid person, nurse or doctor. A man came running over and told me that he worked for the British Red Cross and that he had a first aid kit in his car. He told me that he would look after the injured people but that he would need an assistant. I asked a lady if she would help him and she said that she would. I then decided that I needed to call the emergency services and went to use my mobile phone.

At this point a man pointed out to me that if I used the orange emergency phone it would get through quicker and the operator would be able to locate exactly where the accident was. I asked him if he would call the emergency services on the orange phone, as he appeared to know exactly what he was doing. I noticed a lady sat on the embankment next to the hard shoulder crying and she appeared to be a bit shocked.

I asked an onlooker if he would mind sitting with her and talking to her until the ambulance got there. I thought this was important so that she felt supported and not alone.

Once that was done, the remaining onlookers and I decided to work as a team to remove the debris lying in the road, which would hinder the route for the oncoming emergency service vehicles."

Top tip

- Provide a response that is both concise and flows in a logical sequence.

PART 4 - HOW WAS IT DECIDED HOW THINGS WERE GOING TO BE DONE?

"I decided to take the initiative and get everyone working as a team. I asked the people to let me know what their particular strengths were. One person was first aid trained and so he had the task of attending to the injured. Everyone agreed that we needed to work together as a team in order to achieve the task."

PART 5 - WHAT DID YOU DO TO ENSURE THE TEAM WERE ABLE TO GET THE RESULT THEY WANTED?

"I took control of a deteriorating situation and got everybody who was stood around doing nothing involved. I made sure I asked if anybody was skilled in certain areas such as first aid and used the people who had experience, such as the man who knew about the orange emergency telephones.

I also kept talking to everybody and asking them if they were OK and happy with what they were doing. I tried my best to co-ordinate the people with jobs that I felt needed to be done as a priority."

Top tip

- Try to include details that demonstrate how your actions had a positive impact on the result.

PART 6 - WHAT BENEFIT DID YOU SEE FOR YOURSELF IN WHAT YOU DID?

"The benefit overall was for the injured people, ensuring that they received treatment as soon as possible. However, I did feel a sense of achievement that the team had worked well together even though we had never met each other before. I also learnt a tremendous amount from the experience.

At the end we all shook hands and talked briefly and there was a common sense of achievement amongst everybody that we had done something positive. Without each other we wouldn't have been able to get the job done."

Top tip

- Try to explain that the benefit was positive.

SAMPLE QUESTION NUMBER 5

During very difficult circumstances, police officers must be able to remain calm and act logically and decisively. Please describe a situation when you have been in a very challenging or difficult situation and had to make a decision where other people disagreed with you. You will be assessed in this question on how positively you reacted in the face of adversity and challenge.

PART 1 - TELL US ABOUT THE SITUATION AND WHY YOU FELT IT WAS DIFFICULT.

"Whilst working in my current position as a sales person I was the duty manager for the day as my manager had gone sick. It was the week before Christmas and the shop was very busy.

During the day the fire alarm went off and I started to ask everybody to evacuate the shop, which is our company policy. The alarm has gone off in the past but the normal manager usually lets people stay in the shop whilst he finds out if it's a false alarm.

This was a difficult situation because the shop was very busy, nobody wanted to leave and my shop assistants were disagreeing with me in my decision to evacuate the shop. Some of the customers were becoming irate as they were in the changing rooms at the time."

Top tip

- For questions of this nature you will need to focus on the core competency that relates to resilience. Remember to use keywords and phrases in your responses that match the core competencies being assessed.

PART 2 - WHO DISAGREED WITH YOU AND WHAT DID THEY SAY OR DO?

"Both the customers and my shop assistants were disagreeing with me. The customers were saying that it was appalling that they had to evacuate the shop and that they would complain to the head office about it.

The sales staff were trying to persuade me to keep everybody inside the shop and saying that it was most probably a false alarm as usual. I was determined to evacuate everybody from the shop for safety reasons and would not allow anybody to deter me from my aim.

The safety of my staff and customers was at the forefront of my mind even though it wasn't at theirs."

Top tip

- Do not become aggressive or confrontational when dealing with people who disagree with you. Remain calm at all times but be resilient in your actions if it is right to do so.

PART 3 - WHAT DID YOU SAY OR DO?

"Whilst remaining calm and in control I shouted at the top of my voice that everybody was to leave, even though the sound of the alarm was reducing the impact of my voice. I then had to instruct my staff to walk around the shop and tell everybody to leave whilst we investigated the problem.

I had to inform one member of staff that disciplinary action would be taken against him if he did not co-operate. Eventually, after I kept persisting, everybody began to leave the shop. I then went outside with my members of staff, took a roll call and awaited the Fire Brigade to arrive."

Top tip

- Remember to be in control at all times and remain calm. These are qualities that good police officers will possess.

PART 4 - TELL US HOW THIS SITUATION MADE YOU FEEL INITIALLY.

"At first I felt a little apprehensive and under pressure but determined not to move from my position as I knew 100% that it was the right one. I was disappointed that my staff did not initially help me but the more I persisted the more confident I became.

This was the first time I had been the manager of the shop so I felt that this situation tested my courage and determination. By remaining calm I was able to deal with the situation far more effectively."

Top tips

- Do not say that you felt angry and do not use words that are confrontational.

- By staying calm you will be able to deal with situations far more effectively.

PART 5 - HOW DID YOU FEEL IMMEDIATELY AFTER THE INCIDENT?

"I felt good because I had achieved my aim and I had stood by my decision. It made me feel confident that I could do it again and deal with any difficult situation. I now felt that I had the courage to manage the shop better and had proven to myself that I was capable of dealing with difficult situations.

I had learnt that staying calm under pressure improves your chances of a successful outcome dramatically."

SAMPLE QUESTION NUMBER 6

Police Officers must deliver an excellent service to the public. It is also important that they build good working relationships with the public and other stakeholders. Describe a situation when you had to deal with someone who was disappointed with the level of service they received. Try to use an occasion where you had contact with that person over a period of time or on a number of different occasions in order to rectify the problem.

PART 1 – DESCRIBE THE SITUATION AND WHY YOU THINK THE PERSON WAS NOT HAPPY.

"Whilst working as a sales person in my current job, I was approached by an unhappy customer. He explained to me, in an angry manner, that he had bought a pair of running trainers for his daughter's birthday the week before. When she unwrapped her present the morning of her birthday she noticed that one of the training shoes was a size 6 whilst the other one was a size 7.

Understandably he was not happy with the level of service that he had received from our company. The reason for his dissatisfaction was that his daughter had been let down on her birthday and as a consequence he then had to travel back into town to sort out a problem that should not have occurred in the first place."

Top tips

- In order to respond to this type of question accurately you will need to study and understand the core competency that relates to customer focus.

- Make sure you answer the question in two parts. Describe the situation and then explain why the person was not happy.

PART 2 – EXPLAIN WHAT YOU DID IN RESPONSE TO HIS CONCERNS.

"Immediately I tried to diffuse his anger by telling him that I fully understood his situation and that I would feel exactly the same if I was in his position. I promised him that I would resolve the situation and offered him a cup of tea

or coffee whilst he waited for me to address the problem. This appeared to have the effect of calming him down and the tone in his voice became friendlier.

I then spoke to my manager and explained the situation to him. I suggested that maybe it would be a good idea to replace the running shoes with a new pair (both the same size) and also refund the gentleman in full as a gesture to try to make up for our mistake. The manager agreed to my suggestion and so I returned to the gentleman concerned and explained what we proposed to do for him. He was delighted with the good will offer and appeared to calm down totally.

We then went over to the checkout to refund his payment and replace the running shoes. At this point I took down the gentleman's address and telephone number, which is company policy for any goods returned for refund or exchange. The man then left the shop happy with the service he had received.

The following day I telephoned the gentleman at home to check that everything was OK with the running shoes and he told me that his daughter was delighted. He also informed me that despite the initial bad experience he would still use our shop in the future."

Top tip

- Remember that customer focus is an important element of the role of a police officer. You must focus on the needs of the customer at all times.

PART 3 – HOW DID YOU KNOW THAT THE PERSON WAS HAPPY WITH WHAT YOU DID?

"I could detect a change in his behaviour as soon as I explained that I sympathised with his situation. Again, when I offered him a cup of tea or coffee I detected a change in his behaviour once more.

The tone in his voice became less agitated and angry so I took advantage of this situation and tried even harder to turn his bad experience with us into a positive one. When we offered him the refund along with the replacement of the running shoes his attitude changed again but this time he appeared to be satisfied.

Finally, when I telephoned him the following day he was so happy that he said he would come back to us again despite the initial poor level of service."

Top tip

- In your response to this part of the question try to indicate that you followed up your actions by contacting the person to see if they were satisfied with what you did for them.

PART 4 – IF YOU HADN'T ACTED LIKE YOU DID WHAT DO YOU THINK THE OUTCOME WOULD HAVE BEEN?

"To begin with I believe the situation would have become even more heated and possibly untenable. His anger or dissatisfaction could have escalated if my attempts to diffuse the situation had not taken place. I also believe that we would have lost a customer and therefore lost future profits and custom for the company. There would have been a high possibility that the gentleman would have taken his complaint higher, either to our head office, trading standards or the local newspaper.

Customer service is important and we need to do everything we can (within reason) to make the level of service we provide as high as possible. I also believe that our reputation could have been damaged as that particular gentleman could have told friends or colleagues not to use our shop in the future, whereas now, he is maybe more inclined to promote us in a positive light instead."

Top tips

- Demonstrate that you have a clear understanding of what would have happened if you had not acted as you did.

- Study the core competency that is relevant to customer focus before answering this question.

- Use keywords and phrases in your response from the core competency that is being assessed.

SAMPLE QUESTION NUMBER 7

Police officers must be organised and manage their own time effectively. Please describe a situation when you were under pressure to carry out a number of tasks at the same time.

Tell us what you had to do, which things were a priority and why.

"Whilst working for a sales company as a manager I had 4 important tasks to complete on the last working day of every month. These tasks included stocktaking reports, approving and submitting the sales reps' mileage claims, auditing the previous month's accounts and planning the strategy for the following month's activity.

My first priority was always to approve and submit the sales reps' mileage claims. If I did not get this right or failed to get them submitted on time the reps would be out of pocket when they received their payslip. This would in turn affect morale and productivity within the office. The second task to complete would be the stocktaking reports.

This was important to complete on time as if I missed the deadline we would not have sufficient stock for the following month and therefore there would be nothing to sell and customers would not receive their goods on time. The third task would be the strategy for the following month. This was usually a simple task but still important as it would set out my plan for the following month's activities.

Finally I would audit the accounts. The reason why I would leave this task until the end is that they did not have to be submitted to Head Office until the 14th day of the month and therefore I had extra time to complete this task and ensure that I got it right the first time."

Top tip

- Try to demonstrate that you have excellent organisation skills and that you can cope with the demands and pressures of the job.

SAMPLE QUESTION NUMBER 8

Police officers must be capable of communicating effectively with lots of different people, both verbally and in writing.

Please explain a situation when you had to tell an individual or a group of people something that they may have found difficult or distressing. You will be assessed on how well you delivered the message and also on what you took into account when speaking to them.

PART 1 – WHO WERE THE PEOPLE AND WHAT DID YOU HAVE TO TELL THEM?

"The people involved were my elderly next door neighbours. They had a cat that they had looked after for years and they were very fond of it. I had to inform them that their cat had just been run over by a car in the road."

PART 2 – WHY DO YOU THINK THEY MAY HAVE FOUND THE MESSAGE DIFFICULT OR DISTRESSING?

"I was fully aware of how much they loved their cat and I could understand that the message I was about to tell them would have been deeply distressing. They had cherished the cat for years and to suddenly lose it would have been a great shock to them."

PART 3 – HOW DID YOU DELIVER THE MESSAGE?

"To begin with I knocked at their door and ask calmly if I could come in to speak to them. Before I broke the news to them I made them a cup of tea and sat them down in a quiet room away from any distractions. I then carefully and sensitively told them that their cat had passed away following an accident in the road. At all times I took into account their feelings and I made sure I delivered the message sensitively and in a caring manner."

PART 4 - BEFORE YOU DELIVERED YOUR MESSAGE, WHAT DID YOU TAKE INTO ACCOUNT?

"I took into account where and when I was going to deliver the message. It was important to tell them in a quiet room away from any distractions so that they could grieve in peace. I also took into account the tone in which I delivered the message and I also made sure that I was sensitive to their feelings. I also made sure that I would be available to support them after I had broken the news."

Top tips

- Read the question carefully and make sure you answer every element of it.
- Read the core competency that is relevant to effective communication before providing a response to this question.

You may find on the application form that some of the questions are based around different core competencies. If this is the case then simply apply the same process of trying to match the core competencies by using keywords and phrases in your responses.

Questions based around your reasons and motivations for wanting to become a police officer

In addition to the standard core competency based questions, you may be asked additional questions that are centred around your motivations for wanting to become a police officer with this particular police force.

On the following pages I have provided a number of different questions and sample responses to assist you. Please remember that the responses provided here, and in other parts of this guide, are for guidance purposes only. The responses you provide on your application form must be based around your own individual circumstances, beliefs and circumstances.

SAMPLE QUESTION NUMBER 1

How long have you been thinking about becoming a police officer and what has attracted your attention to the role?

"I have been considering a career as a police officer ever since I started my current sales manager job approximately 7 years ago. I enjoy working in a customer-focused environment and thrive on providing high levels of service to customers. I have always been aware that the police officer's role is demanding, hard work and highly challenging but the rewards of such a job are what attracted my attention in the first place.

The opportunity to work as part of an efficient team and work towards providing the community with an effective service would be highly rewarding and satisfying."

Top tips

- It is not advisable to state that you have only just become interested recently. Candidates who have been seriously thinking about the job for a while will potentially score higher marks.

- Try to demonstrate in your response that you have studied the role carefully and that you believe your skills are suited to being a police officer.

- Those candidates who state that they are attracted solely to the 'catching criminals' side of the role will not score high.

- Read the core competencies and the job description carefully before responding to this question.

- Never be critical of a previous employer.

SAMPLE QUESTION NUMBER 2

What have you done to prepare for this application?

"I have carried out a great deal of research to ascertain whether I am suitable for the role of a police officer and also to find out whether this career would suit my career aspirations. I have studied in depth the police officer core competencies to ensure that I can meet the expectations of this Police Force. I have also carried out extensive research before applying to this particular Police Force as opposed to just applying to any force and hoping that I just get in.

My research began on the Internet through the official police service websites, before finally studying this particular force's website. I have also spoken to current serving police officers at my local station to ask about the role of a working police officer and how it affects their social life.

Finally, I have discussed my intentions with my immediate family to ensure that I have their full support and encouragement."

Top tip

- Preparation is crucial to your success. The police want to know how much preparation you have done and also the type of preparation. If you have carried out plenty of in depth and meaningful preparation then it demonstrates to them that you are very serious about wanting this job. Those applicants who carry out little or no preparation may be simply 'going through the motions'.

FURTHER SAMPLE APPLICATION FORM QUESTIONS AND ANSWERS

During this next section of the guide I have provided you with a host of different sample questions and sample answers. I have varied the types of questions and responses in order to try and cater for the different questions that form part of the application form.

Please note: the responses that are contained within this guide are not to be copied or duplicated in any manner; they are for illustration and guidance purposes only. It is vital that you complete your own form using answers to the questions that are based on your own unique and individual circumstances.

EFFECTIVE COMMUNICATION

EFFECTIVE COMMUNICATION — Q1

It is vitally important that police officers communicate ideas and information effectively, both verbally and in writing.

Please describe a specific situation when you have communicated ideas or information effectively to another person or group of people.

What was the situation and what were the ideas or information you had to communicate?

While at university I found myself in a classroom situation where I was teaching 10 year olds. The children were coming into the university for a PE lesson and I had to take that lesson the university sports hall. My ideas included speaking to the children with a softer voice and coming down to their level so that I was not intimidating towards them.

How did you make sure that you communicated effectively and that your message was understood?

As the pupils were of a very young age I had to be wary of how I spoke to them and how I put my message across. I had to speak with a friendly voice so that the children would not be intimidated. I also had to take note of the different abilities the children had. For example, when some of the children were struggling, I took my time to explain to them how to complete the tasks that had been set for them. I stopped the lesson now and again to make sure the children were having fun and that they understood what they were doing.

What was particularly good or effective about how you dealt with the situation /people involved?

I felt that I communicated with the children in a clear, calm and concise way which led to them being able to understand me clearly. I spoke calmly which gave them the confidence to ask me for help if they required any. When needed I also utilised demonstrations to show them how to do the specific tasks. I also used visual communication skills to aid in my presentations which was particularly useful.

I also used a whistle to communicate with the children. I stated to them beforehand that I would blow the whistle once for the activity to begin and when I blew it twice I wanted the children to stop what they were doing and sit down.

What difficulties did you experience and how did you overcome them?

I encountered many difficulties when teaching the young children. I had to constantly make sure the children were having fun and not getting bored, while still educating them. To overcome this, I set the children some very simple passing drills and would only ask them to continue the same drills for a couple of minutes. This meant that they had enough time to learn the skills but also not get bored of doing the same task for too long. Another difficulty was that some of the children were very shy and were too scared to ask for help if they found a certain task difficult. I was constantly monitoring the children and if I found a pupil struggling I would go over to them and help them one to one by explaining calmly and clearly.

What was the outcome?

The outcome was that all the children had fun and they successfully learned the basic passing and shooting skills of football. At the end we had a short game and the children really enjoyed it as I gained excellent feedback from the teachers and helpers. The children also benefited from my instruction as they appeared far more confident in their own abilities following the lesson.

EFFECTIVE COMMUNICATION — Q2

It is vitally important that police officers communicate ideas and information effectively, both verbally and in writing.

Please describe a specific situation when you have communicated ideas or information effectively to another person or group of people.

What was the situation and what were the ideas or information you had to communicate?

I had to communicate and instruct how to effectively make an arrest to student special constables, clearly and confidently in line with national policing policy as my role as officer safety trainer.

How did you make sure that you communicated effectively and that your message was understood?

I structured the lesson to clearly show all pupils how to carry out the correct procedure. Using examples and demonstrations and confidently explaining the policy and reasoning behind why it must be done this way. Then, summarising the procedure and checking to make sure everyone understood.

What was particularly good or effective about how you dealt with the situation/people involved?

By structuring the lesson I considered the needs of the whole audience, communicating clearly, demonstrating and then asking the pupils to carry out the procedure themselves to ensure they understood. One student was struggling with understanding fully this technique, so I adapted my teaching style and broke down the instructions for their needs ensuring they understood without making the individual uncomfortable in front of others.

What difficulties did you experience and how did you overcome them?

During re-demonstrating to the pupil that needed further assistance, a few within the group became unfocused and started to behave inappropriately and ill-disciplined. To take control of the situation I spoke calm and firmly with authority to express their behaviour was inappropriate and bring the group back to focus on the procedure.

What was the outcome?

The behaviour ceased and the entire group finished the course with a full understanding of the procedure and policy giving them the confidence to use it in the line of their duty.

EFFECTIVE COMMUNICATION — Q3

It is vitally important that police officers communicate ideas and information effectively, both verbally and in writing.

Please describe a specific situation when you have communicated ideas or information effectively to another person or group of people.

What was the situation and what were the ideas or information you had to communicate?

I attended a meeting in which we were to discuss the company's sales objective for the year. I was given a five minute time slot to explain my suggestions on how to promote the company.

How did you make sure that you communicated effectively and that your message was understood?

To make the best effort for my ideas to be understood I put together a short PowerPoint presentation which had keys points highlighted. I spoke to the group clearly by only explaining the relevant points of the presentation.

What was particularly good or effective about how you dealt with the situation /people involved?

I dealt with the situation by preparing properly for the meeting. I clearly explained my ideas and created a good presentation.

What difficulties did you experience and how did you overcome them?

I experienced difficulties during the meeting because some members of the group did not agree with my proposals and often challenged my ideas. I dealt with this by keeping calm and fully answering their questions until they were satisfied with my ideas.

What was the outcome?

The outcome of the meeting was positive as the group felt that I had brought some good ideas to the meeting. They felt that I had prepared well and explained my ideas properly.

EFFECTIVE COMMUNICATION — Q4

Police Constables are often in face-to-face situations where effective verbal communications skills are essential

Describe a face-to-face situation when your verbal communication skills have been tested.

Whilst I was employed with the RSPCA, one of my tasks as Duty Manager was to inform a colleague called Jane that a dog with whom she had built up a strong relationship with had been put to sleep. All the team had grown fond of the dog and worked hard to address some of his behavioural issues in the hope that he could be safely re-homed. Unfortunately, it became apparent that this would not be possible and after discussions it was agreed that the only option was for him to be humanely put to sleep in the near future. Jane became distressed during the discussions, and although acknowledged what was to be the inevitable outcome, she found the decision difficult to accept.

In what way were your skills tested?

I knew from previous experiences that Jane would find the information difficult to accept. My skills were tested as I knew that Jane would understandably react negatively to the information I was providing her with. I was aware that the centre was very noisy which was going to make communication difficult. As soon as Jane realised the dog was no longer with us she became distressed, cried and declared angrily that it had been the wrong decision. Jane was absorbed in her grief and initially unable or unwilling to listen to anything I wanted to say to her.

What did you do to resolve the situation?

I remained calm and guided Jane to a quieter, more private area. She was sobbing, absorbed in her grief. I talked to her softly in a slow, caring tone, using simple words, sounds and sentences. By using these communicative techniques I was able to calm her down effectively. I gave her the time to verbalise her anger and hurt in a controlled environment. Initially I said very little and was aware of using eye contact, nodding and facial expression to convey my concern and understanding whilst encouraging her to continue. I listened carefully without judging or being influenced by my own perception of the situation. I checked my understanding of her views and feelings by paraphrasing some of what she said. When asked what my view was of the situation I felt able to convey it clearly and honestly, whilst considering her feelings. I acknowledged her distress and gave a positive message of how everyone had given the dog their best effort. I assured her that sadly, the outcome had been the only feasible solution.

What was the outcome?

I was able to manage my own emotions by standing back, evaluating the circumstances and rationalising the decision. This allowed me to concentrate and communicate in a professional, yet caring and sensitive manner with Jane. Despite differences in our perception and views of the situation, by being genuinely concerned about how Jane was feeling, and actively listening I was able to see the situation from her point of view, enabling me to empathise and address some of her concerns in an appropriate manner. Jane later said that she appreciated the manner in which I had handled her grief, and being given the time to discuss, consider and come to terms with what had happened.

PERSONAL RESPONSIBILITY

PERSONAL RESPONSIBILITY — Q1

It is vitally important that police officers take personal responsibility for making things happen and achieving results.

Describe a specific situation when you have persevered or have had to put in extra effort in order to complete a task.

Why was it necessary to perceive or put in extra effort?

As a student, finishing my degree was a big challenge in which I had to persevere with. I could have left school straight away to earn money, however I needed to think of the future. I could get a job as soon as I finished school or I could go to University and give myself more opportunities in the long run. I had to put in extra effort in order to get the grades I needed to obtain my degree.

How did you approach the situation and make sure you completed the task?

I had always remembered my end goal. How I would feel when I achieved my degree. I always kept in mind the opportunities I was giving myself for the future. In ten years I wanted to be doing something I had a passion for. I wanted a career and not just a job. If I set myself a goal in which I have full control of, then there is no reason to fail. To complete the task I made a revision and work timeline. I planned how much extra-curricular work I would do whilst not at university. I arranged this around time to relax and spend time with friends etc. This usually meant that after university I would spend a couple of hours at home going over the material I had learned in lectures and seminars.

What was particularly good or effective about how you dealt with the situation?

Overall, I believe my planning was very effective. I believe that there is no reason to fail something which I have full control of. As long as I kept this in mind I could maintain motivation. I planned what extra work I would do while at home. I could sit down and revise over the work I had learned through the day. This meant that when the time came for exams, I had already revised most of the work over the previous months. Also, as I planned to leave time for socialising and free time, it meant that I wasn't so bogged down with work that I became demotivated and lost interest. It meant that I planned my days very well so I looked forward to spending time with friends, but I also looked forward to getting back to my revision.

What did you consider when dealing with the situation?

I considered that the only person who could take responsibility for the future was me. With this at the forefront of my mind I set about planning how to approach the situation. I considered how much time I would need to revise fully, whether I would need any resources to complete the revision and also what the end goal was going to be.

What difficulties did you experience and how did you overcome them?

It was difficult not being able to spend as much time socialising with friends as I didn't have the time or the money. I did have a part time job but that was just to cover living and university costs. Doing my degree and thinking of the future I was giving myself more opportunities for the future. I focused entirely on the end goal and maintain self-motivation throughout.

PERSONAL RESPONSIBILITY — Q2

It is vitally important that police officers take personal responsibility for making things happen and achieving results.

Describe a specific situation when you have persevered or have had to put in extra effort in order to complete a task.

Why was it necessary to persevere or put in extra effort?

The owner of the butchers I work in was absent during the Christmas period. I voluntarily took on the role and responsibilities of running the shop and ensuring all orders were completed on time and to good standards. I ensured that our customers were not disappointed and the business ran smoothly.

How did you approach the situation and make sure that you completed the task?

I approached the situation by being self-motivated and I took personal responsibility to prioritise the tasks that needed doing. I also delegated to other staff whilst overseeing the on-going situation to ensure it was carried out to a satisfactory standard. I also approached the situation by making sure everyone worked to their strengths and weaknesses. This ensured that we met all deadlines and carried out all work to a very good standard.

What was particularly good or effective about how you dealt with the situation?

By taking personal responsibility I used my organisational skills and integrity of all persons to make decisions and resolve all tasks, no matter how routine. This meant that all tasks were completed and all deadlines were met successfully.

What did you consider when dealing with the situation?

I considered all staff members strengths and weaknesses, including my own. I also considered the need to take initiative in order to complete any tasks myself, no matter how small. I also ensured that I worked within time constraints and also adhered to company policies so that everyone was safe.

What difficulties did you experience and how did you overcome them?

Some tasks were almost impossible to complete with the low staffing available, which meant having to reorganise tasks. This also meant a requirement for me to work overtime. I overcame the difficulties by voluntarily working extra hours and also staying focused and persevering on the tasks in hand.

PERSONAL RESPONSIBILITY — Q3

It is vitally important that police officers take personal responsibility for making things happen and achieving results.

Describe a specific situation when you have persevered or have had to put in extra effort in order to complete a task.

Why was it necessary to perceive or put in extra effort?

I had to quickly issue legal action against a client who had defrauded our company. I had to collate a huge amount of information in two days. It was necessary for me persevere and act quickly as there was a chance the client could leave the Country and take all their money and assets.

How did you approach the situation and make sure you completed the task?

I approached the situation by organising myself properly and spoke to legal experts to understand what action needed to be taken. I made sure I completed the task by working extra hours before and after work. I also did not take a lunch break until the task was completed on time.

What was particularly good or effective about how you dealt with the situation?

I dealt with the situation effectively by making sure I consulted the correct legal people. I was also proactive and put in extra hours before and after work.

What did you consider when dealing with the situation?

I had to consider several factors such as ensuring the task was completed by the deadline. I had to manage my time properly as I had other tasks to complete as well. I also had to keep my management informed of my progress as this would help them to make important decisions on the fraud.

What difficulties did you experience and how did you overcome them?

I experienced difficulties when trying to complete my task such as trying to balance my other work and ensuring that it was completed as well. I overcame this by organising myself properly and working harder. I also experienced that there was a lot of information to collate in a short space of time, I overcome this be working extra hours before and after work, I also worked through my lunch break.

RESILIENCE

RESILIENCE — Q1

It is vitally important that police officers show reliability and resilience, even in difficult circumstances.

Describe a specific example of a time when you have found yourself in a difficult or challenging situation.

What was the situation and why was it difficult or challenging?

I was taking part in my final Gold Duke of Edinburgh's award final expedition. We were on our third day of the five day expedition and we were due to climb one of the Yorkshire Dales three peaks Pen-y-Ghent. However, it was a very windy, rainy and foggy day so we needed to decide whether it was safe as one member of our group was starting to have big doubts about being able to navigate the route.

How did you respond and deal with the situation?

During the day we had made excellent time and were an hour ahead of time, so we decided to have a 45-minute break at the bottom of Pen-y-Ghent so we could recover and take on fluids and carbohydrates. We all sat down and we decided how we were going to continue on with the route. I decided to take charge and I stated to the group that I would navigate the route as I was the strongest navigator. I allocated a colleague who was the most competent with a compass. This way we had two people navigating; me using the map and a colleague using the compass. I constantly made sure that the other members of the group new exactly where we were at all times reassuring them that we were always on track.

What was particularly good or effective about how you dealt with the situation/people involved?

I used each member of the group's strength effectively, so that the group functioned fantastically during the hardest part of the expedition. I was the strongest navigator so I decided to navigate the hardest part of the route; this made the group confident that we would be successful in completing the route ahead. Also, a colleague navigated the route using bearings as a backup to my navigating. This is because it was a very foggy day and hard to spot objects in the distance that would help in my navigation. The bearings would be a backup so that we were always going in the right direction for when the fog became too thick for us to see the path.

What did you consider when dealing with the situation?

When dealing with the situation I firstly had to consider the safety of the team. As it was getting very foggy I had to determine whether it was safe enough for us to continue. I also had to consider that certain members of the group may not be as fit as others within the group so I suggested that we should walk the pace of the slowest walker so that no one would get left behind and lost in the fog. However, I also needed to consider the time it would take for us to get to our destination walking at this pace and whether or not we would get their before night fall. It was a priority for us to get to our destination before night fall. We did not have the equipment available to carry out the expedition in the dark.

What difficulties did you encounter and how did you deal with them?

I encountered a few difficulties when navigating in the fog. Although I was constantly marking our location on my map, due to the fog, I occasionally became confused as to our exact location and which path to take at crossroads. This is why I made a team member navigate using bearings. When I became stuck, he could get us on track using the bearings we had pre-planned using the compass. I ensured a focused, resilient and determined approach at all times.

RESILIENCE — Q2

It is vitally important that police officers show reliability and resilience, even in difficult circumstances.

Describe a specific example of a time when you have found yourself in a difficult or challenging situation.

What was the situation and why was it difficult or challenging?

Whilst on duty I was called to a domestic where a female stated she had been assaulted by her husband. The situation was made difficult due to the highly emotional teenage children not wishing for their father to be arrested.

How did you respond and deal with situation?

I took control of the situation by keeping calm and focused, separating the two parents into separate rooms to diffuse conflict and tensions between two parties. Although still receiving aggression from two teenagers who were highly emotional and trying to prevent their father being arrested.

What was particularly good or effective about how you dealt with the situation?

Whilst staying professional throughout I stood firm on my decision that it was necessary to arrest him to prevent further harm to their mother, even though this was unpopular with the teenagers who were highly hostile and provocative towards me due to this.

What did you consider when dealing with the situation?

After consideration it was necessary to arrest husband although the teenagers were confrontational I stood firm to my decision knowing it was correct and whilst resisting pressure from teenagers. I ensured that I used the minimum force appropriate whilst staying in control of the situation.

What difficulties did you experience and how did you overcome them?

It was highly emotional situation. By staying calm and avoiding inappropriate emotions I resisted coming to a rash solution. This enabled me to find the right outcome and ensure correct procedure was done professional.

RESILIENCE — Q3

It is vitally important that police officers show reliability and resilience, even in difficult circumstances.

Describe a specific example of a time when you have found yourself in a difficult or challenging situation.

What was the situation and why was it difficult or challenging?

A client had just seriously breached our company agreement by banking a cheque that did not belong to him. I had to make a difficult decision of placing the client's account on stop and preventing further payments being sent to him. This proved to be a challenging situation, as no payments meant the client would be unable meet their financial obligations.

How did you respond and deal with situation?

I quickly dealt with the situation by e-mailing all the directors informing them of my decision. I also issued a letter to the client detailing the breach. I also spoke to the client and informed them that they were to pay back the money immediately.

What was particularly good or effective about how you dealt with the situation?

I believe that due to the fact I acted decisively meant the situation could be resolved quickly and with no damage caused to the client's business. I also kept the client informed of any decisions made on a regular basis.

What did you consider when dealing with the situation?

When dealing with the situation I considered the effects on the client's business and that if the account was on stop for a long period of time then it would have detrimental effects, for example the client not being able to pay their staff's wages.

What difficulties did you experience and how did you overcome them?

I experienced a number of difficulties when dealing with the situation. One difficulty was that some of my company directors did not agree with my decision. I overcame this by explaining my reasons behind my decision and keeping them informed with any developments. Another difficulty I had was keeping the account on hold. I overcame this by speaking to the client on a regular basis and requesting the money to be repaid. The client did repay the funds and the account was reopened resolving the situation.

FLEXIBILITY

FLEXIBILITY — Q1

Flexibility is a key skill required of a Police Constable.

Describe a time when you had to be flexible or deal with change.

I was employed for several months as a waitress in a popular bistro, which was situated in the centre of Brisbane. During a busy lunchtime a heated argument erupted resulting in the Chef walking out of the premises, closely followed by the Duty Manager. The bistro was full and some customers were seated waiting on the food they had ordered and others were queuing to place orders.

What action did you take?

The team had to react quickly to the unexpected situation. I asked the till operator if she was happy to continue taking orders whilst I initiated a brief discussion in the kitchen with the remaining staff on how best to proceed. Skills and experience were considered and some roles and responsibilities were changed and shared. I volunteered to primarily take orders and serve food as it was felt that that was the area I was best suited to being able to retain a calm and professional composure with the customers. I also helped the coffee operator and washed dishes depending on the demands on the service.

What was the outcome?

All customers were happy with the service they received, including the quality of the food and several who had witnessed the Chef leaving complimented the team on their management of the situation. I was a willing member of a team who adapted well to the altered circumstances and rose to the challenge to meet customers' expectations. I felt I promoted a positive attitude to the unexpected circumstances to other team members. I did not get stressed or complain about the situation but thrived on the challenge.

RESPECT FOR RACE AND DIVERSITY

RESPECT FOR RACE AND DIVERSITY — Q1

It is vitally important that police officers demonstrate consideration and respect for others.

Describe a specific situation when you have been required to demonstrate sensitivity or have shown understanding of the needs/ views of another person or group of people. In your response to this question you may draw on your past experience when you have dealt with others who are different from you in any way.

Why was it necessary to demonstrate sensitivity or show understanding?

Whilst working in a nightclub, I dealt with people from all walks of life. An incident in the past has been when a young lady from a different background had become drunk and had lost all her friends causing her to be very upset and frightened. As she was intoxicated, it made her vulnerable. I had to show understanding otherwise the matter would have escalated due to the language barrier and the different cultures we were from. She would have become more upset and frightened. I had to keep her calm and say that I would do my best to find her friends or at least make sure she got home safe.

How did you deal with the situation and how did you make sure you demonstrated sensitivity or showed understanding?

I dealt with the situation by getting her some water and getting her to calm down and explain what had happened in a slow manner so that I could understand. We then went back to where she had last seen her friends to see if we could find them. When we couldn't find them, we rang both her friends and arranged for them to meet her.

Throughout the time I spent with the young lady I did my best to keep her calm. I did this by being understanding and reassuring her that I would either find her friends or make sure that she would get home safe. I did not lecture her about the situation but instead sympathised with her. I had to keep her thinking practically so that we would find the people that she was out with.

What was particularly good about how you dealt with the situation/people involved?

My biggest asset is the ability to always remain calm. It has a calming influence on people and people mirror the behaviour of those they are speaking with. I managed to stop the young lady crying and instead get her thinking in more of a practical way. She felt calm and reassured which meant dealing with the matter was a lot easier. When her initial panic stage had passed after I had reassured her everything would be fine, she started having a little joke about how in a few days herself and her friends would look back on this and laugh. This showed that I handled the situation perfectly as the young lady was no longer worried and frightened, despite the potential language and cultural barriers.

What did you consider when dealing with the situation?

I considered how the lady must be feeling and how I would want my sister to be treated in a similar situation. I had to think of how best to reassure her that she would be ok. I also considered her needs and respected her culture. I had to consider that the young lady may be a bit embarrassed by her current situation so I decided to take her to a staff only part of the club so she wasn't conscious of everyone looking at her thinking what was wrong. This calmed her down. I kept telling her that everything would be fine and I would reunite her with her friends. I also had to think of how best to find her friends or at least make sure she got home safely. I considered using the police radio at to inform other venues of the situation and to look out for her friends to tell them what had happened.

What difficulties did you encounter and how did you overcome them?

I had to deal with a very upset and intoxicated young lady far away from home; therefore I had to stay calm. A difficulty was getting in contact with her friends. Looking for a specific group of people would be difficult. I decided to use the police radio to notify other venues what the situation was. I took a description of the lady's friends and then radioed this to the other venues. If the group were seen then they would be told by staff what the situation was.

RESPECT FOR RACE AND DIVERSITY — Q2

It is vitally important that police officers demonstrate consideration and respect for others.

Describe a specific situation when you have been required to demonstrate sensitivity or have shown understanding of the needs/ views of another person or group of people. In your response to this question you may draw on your past experience when you have dealt with others who are different from you in any way.

Why was it necessary to determine sensitivity or show understanding?

A gentleman from a different background came into the butcher shop where I worked. The shop manager was rude and abrupt to the male as the male could not speak fluent English. Due to this the male walked out of the store upset and offended at this behaviour. It was necessary to show understanding and sensitivity as the man was from a different background and, as such, it would have been difficult for him to understand a new language and culture.

How did you deal with the situation and how did you make sure you demonstrated sensitivity

I was busy at the back of the shop but overheard what had happened. Due to the treatment of the male I decided to pursue him and apologised. I explained my colleague's behaviour was unacceptable and understand that that it was offensive. I explained I would take personal responsibility to ensure his needs were met.

What was particularly good or effective about how you dealt with situation?

I was patient with the male and provided him with support. I also listened and acknowledging his views and opinions whilst later challenging the behaviour of the manager who was aggressive and discriminatory. For this my manager later apologised for his behaviour.

What did you consider when dealing with the situation?

I considered how I would confront my manager, challenging him on his inappropriate attitude. I also considered the feelings and cultural values of the costumer listening to the opinions of both sides.

What difficulties did you experience and how did you overcome them

Apart from the language barrier with the costumer I also had to challenge my manager regarding his inappropriate attitude that I done discreetly away from costumers. I overcame these difficulties by staying calm and considering the feelings and views of both parties.

RESPECT FOR RACE AND DIVERSITY — Q3

It is vitally important that police officers demonstrate consideration and respect for others.

Describe a specific situation when you have been required to demonstrate sensitivity or have shown understanding of the needs/ views of another person or group of people. In your response to this question you may draw on your past experience when you have dealt with others who are different from you in any way.

Why was it necessary to determine sensitivity or show understanding?

I had to demonstrate and explain a presentation to a large group. The presentation was on a Friday afternoon and quite a few members of the group were Muslim and needed to go to prayer at the local mosque. I know that Friday prayers are the most important of the week and it was important not to let the presentation over run or let them leave early.

How did you deal with the situation and how did you make sure you demonstrated sensitivity

I dealt with the situation by letting my Muslim colleagues leave early during the presentation. I also constantly checked the time so they could leave in time for prayer. Before they left I spoke to them outside the meeting room and said I understood they need to leave for prayer; however, they will need to come back and catch up on the remainder of the presentation to which they gladly agreed.

What was particularly good or effective about how you dealt with situation?

I dealt with the situation effectively by not being difficult and preventing them from leaving the meeting early. When I spoke to them I told them I understood they needed to attend afternoon prayer and it was not an issue. I demonstrated that I fully respected their religion and took steps to accommodate their wishes.

What did you consider when dealing with the situation?

I considered that Friday prayers are the most important prayer of the week for the Muslim faith and it was important I did not prevent them from leaving on time. I considered their feelings and took into account the consequences of not allowing them permission to leave the presentation early.

What difficulties did you experience and how did you overcome them

The difficulties I experienced were that some of the group were a little put out that they were allowed to leave early. I explained to the group that it was important they attended afternoon prayer as it was the most important prayer of the week.

TEAMWORK

TEAMWORK — Q1

Police Constables must work as part of a team during their everyday activities.

Describe a situation where you had to work as part of a team to complete a task or achieve a goal.

Whilst volunteering with The Born Free Foundation in Africa I was part of a team, some of whom I had never previously worked with, assisting a Veterinary Surgeon and a Veterinary Nurse in spaying and neutering dogs and cats in a local community building.

How did you contribute to help the team?

I took part in the discussion planning for the event, encouraging quieter members to take part and being aware volunteers were from different countries, cultures and backgrounds. I respected and accepted their different values, opinions and experiences. I made time to get to know other team members. I conveyed my relevant skills, experience and limitations but offered to help in whatever way I could best be utilised, including undertaking some of the less popular tasks. I helped identify possible issues/problems. I volunteered to carry out the tasks of administering antibiotics, anti-inflammatory and rabies medication by injection and applying de-fleeing and de-worming treatments. I carried out these tasks and others which presented having not previously been discussed or allocated. I also helped others with some of their tasks and assisted the Veterinary Nurse when I saw she was struggling to retain her composure when confronting a teenage boy who was kicking his dog following its operation.

What was the result of your actions?

By clearly communicating my relevant skills, experience and limitations, and my offer to carry out whatever tasks would be most beneficial to the team, I helped the team plan the event. My respect of other members' backgrounds and opinions and my encouragement and support of some of the quieter members of the group enabled them to contribute to the discussion and decision-making. At the event, by being aware of how other members of the team were coping and by helping them when appropriate, I feel I contributed to the overall smooth running of the event. By previously making time to get to know other team members I felt we had a stronger bond and had built trust and confidence in each other which helped us work and cooperate better as a team. By assisting the nurse in dealing with the actions of the teenage boy, I helped to diffuse a situation which could have escalated.

What did you learn about teamwork from that experience?

A team needs a coordinator/leader that can communicate effectively and give direction. Team members can be from different countries, cultures, backgrounds and lifestyles but everyone's opinions, values and experiences should be respected and valued. Stronger bonds can be made within a team when members have made an effort to know each other better. I also learned that even if team members had never worked together before, if they know their roles, they can operate effectively. I learned that flexibility is important and the ability to assess situations quickly and react appropriately. Team members should be aware of any support or assistance colleagues might need as well as being aware of when to ask for and accept help themselves. Some of the more routine or less popular tasks all contribute to and are important in achieving the end goal. I also learned that by reviewing how well the task had gone, the team can learn from experiences and strive to improve in the future.

FURTHER QUESTIONS AND ANSWERS

Q. Tell us why you want to become a police officer.

Working in a customer based environment I find the position challenging but enjoy thriving on finding a solution to a problem. Working within a team I have strengthened my ability to be a good team player. I am passionate about protecting the community and keeping it safe. Assisting the community and other services in promoting a stronger, safer well-being to all victims, vulnerable people and society as a whole is something that I very much enjoy. I believe in building relationships and pursuing opportunities to assist and engage vulnerable groups.

Q. Tell us why you have applied to your chosen force.

I have been a special constable for a period of time and also police staff for the police force. I have witnessed a dedicated and striving force and wish to become an officer with this particular police force for this reason.

Q. Tell us in some detail what tasks you expect to be undertaking as a police officer.

I expect to carry out a varied role, including dealing with issues from domestic violence, anti-social behaviour, public order and also ensuring high visibility targeted patrols ensuring crime prevention. Whilst at times dealing with the sensitive matter of sudden deaths on behalf of the coroner.

I will be dealing with victims, criminals and aiding in welfare concerns and assisting other agencies and police forces in many ways. Along with building relationships with the community I will be expected to be a role model for the force.

Q. Tell us what effect being a police officer to have on your social and domestic life.

As already working on a 24 hour shift rota for the police I am aware of the anti-social hours that are involved and that compromises shall have to be done to domestic life. I understand the potential strain it may put on social situations.

Q. What preparation have you undertaken before making this application to ensure that you know what to expect and that you are prepared for the role of police officer.

As a special constable it has prepared me to what to expect of a daily routine of a police officer. I have also spoken to regular officers to understand what is expected as a police officer.

Q. Tell us why you want to become a police officer.

I would love to become a police officer because I like to be faced with new challenges on a daily basis. Working as a team is a vital role in police work and I thrive on working as a team in order to achieve set targets and goals. I also want to make a difference in the community I live in and protect it as best as I can work either in a team or as an individual. I also love problem solving and solving problems would be a huge requirement in the police force hence why I feel I am perfectly suited to the job.

Q. Tell us in some detail what tasks you expect to be undertaking as a police officer.

As a police officer I expect to use clear and effective while working as a team in order to carry out specific tasks given to me. I expect to be required to make effective decisions while problem solving that may have a huge effect on someone or something. I expect to be able to identify problems and the use the skills I have learned in order to gather the information required in order to solve them. I expect to be able to take personal responsibility to make things happen as well as working as a team.

Q. Tell us what effect you expect being a police officer to have on your social and domestic life

I expect being a police officer to have a significant effect on my social and domestic life. My job will always come first and when friends are deciding to go for a night out, I will refuse as I will always make sure I am in a fully fit state for work. Days off will be spent relaxing with my family and not out drinking as this will reduce my ability to do my job to the highest standard I can.

Q. What preparation have you undertaken before making this application to ensure that you know what to expect and that you are prepared for the role of police officer?

I have prepared myself both mentally and physically for the role of a police officer. I have kept myself fit my whole life so I feel I am more than capable of passing any fitness test required. I have also read the role and job description of a police officer to ensure that I have the necessary competencies and attributes to carry out the role to the best of my ability.

Q. Tell us why you want to become a police officer.

I enjoy a varied working environment which the police force provides. I also enjoy helping people and trying to make difference to reduce crime in the community.

Q. Tell us why you have applied to join the British Transport Police and not a regular police force.

The British Transport Police offer a wide degree of challenging roles. It is a unique as it is the only police force that deals with any crime that occurs on the railway network. It is also the only National Police force in the Country.

Q. Tell us in some detail what tasks you expect to be undertaking as a British Transport police officer.

I understand that the BTP are responsible for patrolling and safe keeping the public rail network which other Home Office forces do not undertake. BTP concentrate on issues such as pickpocketing, graffiti and criminal damage that occurs on the rail network.

Q. Tell us who you see as 'customers' and 'stakeholders' of the British Transport Police.

I see the customers of the British Transport Police as members of the public who pay to use the rail network. I see a stakeholder as a person or a company that has an interest, normally financial in a business or project. An example of a stakeholder for British Transport Police would be a train operating company.

Q. Tell us what you know about the current operational practices of the British Transport Police.

I know that the British Transport Police main current operation is to maintain security on the rail network leading up to and including the 2012 Olympic Games in London. I also know that the threat of terrorism is high and a visible presence on the rail network is necessary to provide reassurance to the public. Other priorities include reducing knife crime which is covered by Operation Shield.

Q. What tasks do you expect to undertake as a British Transport Police Officer.

As a British Transport Police officer I expect to undertake a multitude of tasks such as high visibility foot patrols on the rail network and stations, deal with incidents such as thefts, pickpocketing, criminal damage, ticket fare evasion and assaults. I will also be required to respond to major incidents, such as persons under a train and possible terrorist threats. Finally, I will be required to police events such as the 2012 Olympic Games, carnivals, demonstrations and football events.

Q. Tell us what effect you expect being a police officer to have on your social and domestic life.

I understand that a police officer's role requires commitment such as working unsocial hours, weekends and nights. I am also aware that you may be called into work on your rest days at very short notice. This will naturally have an impact on my social and domestic life but I will adjust to meet the requirements of the police force.

Q. How do you think your external friendships will be affected when you become a police officer?

Being a police officer will have on impact on my friendships as I will not be able to see them as often due to the unsocial hours that are part of the police officer role. Outside work I expect to conduct myself and maintain a level of integrity and responsibility that would be expected if I were on duty.

Q. What preparation have you undertaken before making this application to ensure that you know what to expect and that you are prepared for the role of British Transport police officer?

I have researched the role of a British Police officer by looking on the website and speaking with current serving officers. I have also become a Special Constable with the police. Even though the role of a police officer with a regular force compared to a British Transport police officer is different, I have gained invaluable experience on how to deal with situations and the public.

Q. What knowledge, skills, experience or attributes do you use as part of your hobbies or interests that will be useful to you as a Police Constable?

I enjoy the gym, swimming, running and walking. Being comfortable outdoors, fit and strong would assist me in meeting the demands of a Police Constable, both physically and mentally. I am a supportive, encouraging team member who makes time to get to know others. I have calmed situations which could have escalated whilst playing in a hockey team, within crowds of rugby supporters and whilst in nightclubs.

I enjoy socialising and meeting new people; continually building on my interpersonal skills. I respect other people's views regardless of their ethnic origin, age, lifestyle, disability or background and I challenge comments or behaviour that is offensive or discriminatory. I treat people with consideration and dignity. I am committed and self-motivated. I am level headed, cope well under pressure and react quickly and appropriately to unexpected situations. I am honest and act with the highest integrity. I reflect on experiences to help identify areas I can develop and improve on.

Q. What other skills or experience (e.g. driving, languages) will you bring to the role of Police Constable?

I have sound computer skills. I have experience of maintaining accurate, concise and confidential records. I have an awareness of issues affecting communities and have worked closely with the elderly and adults with learning disabilities. I worked in a disciplined environment within the RSPCA where I wore my uniform with pride and met expectations of promoting a positive and professional image. I am familiar with animal welfare legislation and I have experience of working with wild, farm and domestic animals. I have volunteered my time in various charitable organisations and helped with children's horse riding lessons. I have spent several years building on my life and work experiences working with members of the public where I have always been committed to meeting and exceeding their expectations, treating them equally and fairly and thriving on challenges. I feel I have the right character, skills and potential to develop with training into an effective Police Constable.

Q. What are your reasons for applying to this particular Force?

I am proud of and care about the Lothian and Borders area in which I live and genuinely want to work within it. I love the diversity of the people and the area, from rural communities to the city of Edinburgh. I want to be part of the respected, committed, professional team who do a worthwhile job meeting and overcoming the area's varying challenges to create safer communities whilst maintaining national priorities. As Lothian and Borders Police Force is the second largest in Scotland and covers a large, varied geographical area I feel there could be possibilities to experience a wide range of policing roles and move and work within it. I am willing to relocate anywhere within the area.

FINAL TIPS FOR COMPLETING A SUCCESSFUL APPLICATION FORM

Whilst some of the following tips have already been provided within this section, it is important that we provide them again. Your success very much depends on your ability to do the following:

- Read the application form and the guidance notes at least twice before you complete it.

- If possible, photocopy the application form and complete a draft copy first. This will allow you to make any errors or mistakes without being penalised.

- Obtain a copy of the core competencies and have them at your side when completing the form.

- Take your time when completing the form and set aside plenty of time for each question. I recommend that you spend 5 evenings completing the application form breaking it down into manageable portions. This will allow you to maintain high levels of concentration.

- Complete the form in the correct colour ink and follow all instructions very carefully. Your form could be thrown out for simply failing to follow simple instructions.

- Be honest when completing the form and if you are unsure about anything contact the police force for confirmation.

- Try not to make any spelling or grammar errors. You WILL lose marks for poor spelling, grammar and punctuation.

- Try to use keywords and phrases in your responses to the assessable questions that are relevant to the core competencies.

- Get someone to check over your form for errors before you submit it. If they can't read your application form, the assessor probably won't be able to either.

- Take a photocopy of your final completed form before submitting it.

- Try to submit the form well before the closing date. Some forces may operate a cut off point in terms of the number of applications they receive.

- Some forms do get lost in the post so it is advisable that you send it by recorded delivery for peace of mind.

- If your form is unsuccessful ask for feedback, if available. It is important that you learn from your mistakes.

WHAT HAPPENS AFTER I HAVE SENT OFF MY APPLICATION FORM?

Once you have completed and sent off your application form there will be a wait period before you find out whether or not you have been successful. Some forces will only write to you if you have been successful.

Regardless of the above, it is crucial that you start preparing for the assessment centre even before you receive your result. By starting your preparation early you will effectively be giving yourself a 2-3 week advantage over the other applicants. 99% of applicants will wait to receive their result before they start to prepare. This is where you can gain an advantage.

Please note that the information you are about to read may differ from force to force. Make sure you confirm the exact requirements of your particular assessment centre before you start preparing.

how2become

Visit www.how2become.co.uk for more police officer titles:

- How to pass the police officer interview

- Online police officer testing facilities

- How to pass any job interview

- 1-day intensive police officer training courses

www.how2become.co.uk